The Fisherman's Prayer

Also by Pat Neal:

"WildLife" vol. 1

The Fisherman's Prayer

✦

Stories, Poems, and Prayers from the Olympic Peninsula

Pat Neal

Good fishing!

Pat Neal.

iUniverse, Inc.
New York Lincoln Shanghai

The Fisherman's Prayer
Stories, Poems, and Prayers from the Olympic Peninsula

iUniverse books may be ordered through booksellers or by contacting:

iUniverse
2021 Pine Lake Road, Suite 100
Lincoln, NE 68512
www.iuniverse.com
1-800-Authors (1-800-288-4677)

ISBN: 978-0-595-44467-0 (pbk)
ISBN: 978-0-595-69438-9 (cloth)
ISBN: 978-0-595-88794-1 (ebk)

Printed in the United States of America

For Sharon

Then He said, "Throw out your net on the right hand side of the boat, and you'll get plenty of them!" So we did, and couldn't draw in the net because of the weight of the fish, there were so many!

—John 2: 6

Contents

List of Illustrations

Author's Note

These stories may have appeared as columns at one time or another in various newspapers in Washington State.

The True Cost of Fishing

People are always asking me how much it costs to go fishing. The fact that someone would even ask a question like that reveals a deep-rooted, guilt-ridden, shame-based sinkhole of personal problems that's not uncommon among people who fish. One man's obsessive-compulsive hoarding disorder is another man's tackle box collection.

Most anglers are in complete denial over how much they spend on fishing until other members of the family start whining about food or shoes. As a fishing guide and unlicensed relationship counselor, I've seen first-hand the effects of the fishing problem on a free and open society.

The true costs of fishing are paid by all of us. The effects have to include the loss of productivity in business and industry. If you've ever been unlucky enough to work with someone with a fishing problem, then you know how it can affect job performance.

People with fishing problems may spend inordinate amounts of time talking about their disease, even if they *do* show up for work.

All too often, some fishermen will stop production to insist that everyone look at their fish pictures, or make coworkers take time out from their busy day to "check out a dead fish in the back of my truck." Untold hours are wasted listening to those one-that-got-away fables that all have one thing in common: an inbred sense of failure that only makes a bad fishing problem worse. Add up all the other miscellaneous expenses associated with fishing—$1,000 rods, $500 reels, divorce—and you can understand how the negative effects of fishing could stall the economic recovery that made our country so cool.

Someone with a bad fishing problem can't admit to themselves how many fish they did or didn't catch. Just ask any fisherman how many he caught and he'll invariably tell you how many he *hooked.*

Hooking a fish and catching it are two different things. But people with fishing problems often can't tell the difference. On any given body of water, half the fishermen may be hooking imaginary fish or snags they pretend are fish just to impress the other fishermen. Go ahead and ask the average fisherman if he's catching anything. Often, they don't know themselves. If the fishermen can't admit they didn't catch a fish, it's unlikely they'll know how much money they spent not catching it.

To illustrate the true costs of fishing, I dumped my tackle box in the river. As I watched the colorful assortment of lures float away—the ones that didn't immediately sink, anyway—I paused to calculate the value of this experiment. I determined the value of the contents of that tackle box at roughly $500. This figure was determined by an accounting method designed specifically for fishing: fish math.

To apply this form of accounting, each number is rounded off, then multiplied or divided by a factor of two, depending on whom you're talking to.

Still, no amount of money can compare to the human costs of fishing. I did not get this way by myself; I had help. I grew up in a family in which social fishing was acceptable behavior. I began fishing early. Perhaps it was a genetic pre-disposition. We were plunking worms in the Elwha River.

In this enlightened age of catch-and-release fishing, of barb-less hooks on artificial lures, fishing with worms seems like a nightmare straight out of the dark ages. But no … it was even worse than that.

Back then, I'd do anything to get worms—anything, that is, except buy them. Every dime I had went for hooks, line, swivels, and lead sinkers that would get the worms down to the bottom of the river. Worms were easy to find in the spring when it was wet, but by summer, I'd do anything for a worm. A dry August might find me weeding

Mom's flowerbed. She thought I was being a good boy for once, until she found out it was all about the worms.

I regret the many acres of rain forest ecosystem I tore through trying to find worms. Verdant fern, moss, and rock gardens, were ripped apart in a frantic search for just one more fat, happy worm to impale on a sharp hook and toss into a long, still, deep pool. Back then, parents thought nothing of giving a kid a jackknife and telling them to whittle a forked stick to hold the fishing pole until you got a bite.

Then you'd get a bite, as that worm was sucked down by an Elwha River rainbow trout. We thought the Elwha Rainbows looked like steelhead because they were descended from steelhead that were trapped upriver when they built the Elwha Dams. All I know for sure is that those fish would snatch that worm and fly out of the river like a bolt of silver electricity. Once we got the fish to shore, the idea of turning it loose made about as much sense as throwing the fishing pole into the river along with it. Trout was food.

Our parents said we couldn't play with our food. We were supposed to cook it. That's when the same parental guidance that turned us loose on the ecosystem with a jackknife and a hatchet would tell us to go play with matches. We had to build a campfire to cook the fish.

Things were under control at first. It was just harmless family fun, casual social fishing. By age six, I'd caught a twelve-inch rainbow trout. I wanted to catch just one more trout, and then another, and another, until before I knew it, I was wa-a-a-y over my limit. I could not have known at the time I was suffering from a disease they didn't have a name for yet: Fishing Affected Attention Disorder (FAAD). I had all the symptoms; I was messy, physically overactive, and unable to wait my turn or focus on anything but fishing.

It was like a slow-motion train wreck that began on my first day of school. I remember wondering why I was sent to school. After all, fishing season wasn't over yet. They put us in a big room where the teacher babbled on and on, talking about stuff that didn't have *anything* to do with fishing.

When I woke up, it was time for lunch. It was an opportunity to share whatever special treats mom packed in the ol' lunch box, if you knew what was good for you. Some of the classmates had been in grade school for so long, they had started shaving. If you had a problem trading your blackberry pie for a rotten banana, you'd better wolf it down first thing in the morning, before you got on the bus.

Then there was recess, complete with games like "Crack the Whip," "Dutch Knuckles," and "Indian Rope Burn." The teachers didn't care what we did. We figured they were in the basement smoking or something, so no one wanted to bother the teachers unless we couldn't get the bleeding stopped on our own. Before you knew it, a teacher fired a signal shot from an old Luger she'd brought back from the war and recess was over. We'd line up in front of the water fountain, waiting ever-so-patiently. Just when you'd get ready to gulp down a drink, some joker would slam into the end of the line, crushing the unfortunate drinker into the fountain. This was back before bottled water—the late-Pleistocene era, I believe.

We used fountain pens, which launch ink quite a ways once you got them sighted in. If you were inked, you were liable to get pasted, with the gooey white stuff you could never quite wipe off. Mix in the rotten fruit and dirt bags you were constantly getting pelted with, and you could come home from school at least a couple times a week looking like modern art painting.

Discipline was strict. The teachers impacted my self-esteem with large pieces of wood. But really, it wasn't *my* fault that I was misbehaving; these behaviors were just more obnoxious symptoms of FAAD.

Fortunately, FAAD can now be controlled with drugs. Just one pill at the start of the school day, with or without food, and Johnny Rotten becomes a model pupil without the teacher acquiring tennis elbow.

Sure, today's back-to-school drugs may cost more, but aren't our children worth it? For just a few dollars a day, parents can dose their children and keep them from ending up like me. Staring out the school window at the distant hills on the first and last days—and every day in between—with a "gone fishing" sign stamped on my forehead.

After what seemed like a year, the last day of school finally arrived. The teacher said how much she would miss us. Well, that was her story ... as for the rest of us, we'd make every effort to "miss" the classmates all summer—some of them had BB guns and fighting dogs. The best place to miss your classmates all was the Olympic Mountains.

While other kids dreamed of being astronauts or ball players, I wanted to catch every fish in those mountains, three times each. But things did not go as planned. As I mentioned, those were the old days, back before the farms were wiped out. Children were considered farm machinery. There were many fine careers to choose from, and I couldn't wait to get started.

Picking strawberries seemed like easy money. Ahh, to start out early on a summer morning, gorging down an endless row of perfectly ripe berries—that is, until your gut hurt so bad you could not walk upright, which started the endless trip to the outhouse where you usually spotted some loser from school. Which, of course, led to a berry fight.

Even if you couldn't pick berries, you could still get on bucking hay bales. Early on a summer morn, we'd cheerfully trot across the fields, bucking bales into the back of a truck where some t'backy chawin' foreman stacked them in a special way so they wouldn't fall off.

Sometimes the farmer gave us pop breaks. If we were lucky, the farmer's wife would cook a noon meal—always something fancy, like hot dogs and beans. But we didn't care. After a morning haying, we'd eat the shingles off the roof.

After lunch, we might have a boxing match to see who drove the truck.

"You boys work it out," the old farmer would chuckle. Oh, we did. That was the big payoff: to drive to the barn at the end of the day with the truck piled impossibly high with hay. Then pop the clutch at the crest of the hill, dump the crew and half the load, and keep driving.

Even if you couldn't drive a hay truck, you could still drive a log truck. These were the good ol' days, when loggers ruled the Earth, when every kid wanted to hot rod down the highway with 90,000 pounds of attitude.

The old man must have sensed this. He had me do all my log truck driving in the parking lot. I was nuts to quit that job. I could have been head grease monkey by now. But like I said, I was gone fishing. At the time, it was socially acceptable for kids to wander off in the hills camping and fishing. We didn't know at the time that it was a symptom of a more sinister problem.

You hear a lot these days about getting close to nature and camping without leaving a trace. If our fish camps had been any closer to nature, they would have been underground.

I'll never forget camping under a bark shelter. We set a pole frame against a big log and covered the works with slabs of cedar bark. There was a carpet of moss on the floor. It was as snug as a bug in a rug for a while. Until the campfire warmed up the bugs, and they came crawling out of that log in droves. But the bugs were forgotten as soon as the skunk showed up.

As we got older, our camping became fancier. We started using plastic to make shelters. An old shower curtain made a perfect lean-to. They had holes around the edge, and were easy to tie a string to. Until the wind hit and the tent ripped loose and flapped away in the breeze, leaving you to endure the elements wrapped in a plastic ball, praying for morning. No RV-er in the history of camping was ever as glad to see daylight. Then you could get moving to warm up and head upstream for a day of fishing.

Creek fishing the Olympics is a form of mountain climbing where you carry a fishing pole instead of a rope. The goal was not to get just beyond the crowds, but to find bottomless canyons and mountain lakes in which no sane person would fish.

By high school, I was binge fishing, and not with just worms anymore. No, I'd graduated to whatever my so-called fishing friends—fellow FAAD sufferers—would come up with. Bees, corn, maggots … you name it. I knew I'd hit the bottom of the bait bucket when I started using the good stuff: fresh salmon eggs.

Someone gave me a jar of cured salmon eggs. At first, the eggs were free. Then I had to catch more fish to get more eggs so I could catch more fish. It was a vicious cycle that did not stop until I ran out of eggs *and* fish.

I'd find myself wandering from one back-country shelter to another, searching for bait some backpacker was too lazy to carry out. Or I'd journey to a fishing town and try to get a job cleaning fish to get more fish eggs.

Since I became a fishing guide, people have been constantly asking me how much it costs to go fishing. So far, fishing has cost me everything.

How Fishing Laws Are Made

Recently someone asked me, "When does fishing and crabbing season open around here?"

It wasn't their fault; they were tourists. I've lived here my whole life—so far—and have a hard time figuring out the fishing regulations.

It's every angler's duty to understand the fishing laws. No one wants to catch the last fish, and besides, our fish cops are meaner than pepper-sprayed skinheads. They'll be more than happy to explain the difference between a bull trout and a bullhead when they cart you off to the big house for barbecuing an endangered species.

I have spent many years researching the fishing laws in an attempt to translate them into English. The latest research suggests the fishing laws must be a form of primitive code, subject to change without notice, rhyme, or reason. Without a translator, you may require an attorney to understand the fishing laws. It's like we say on the river, "If you cannot afford an attorney, then you probably can't afford to go fishing."

To avoid confusion, I might explain how the fishing laws are invented in the first place. It all starts with the governor of Washington. The governor doesn't fish. The governor knows from hard experience that fishermen are trouble. The fishermen blame the governor for the fishing. It's not the governor's fault; fishermen can't agree on anything among themselves.

The fisheries resource is divided between competing groups of tribal, commercial, and sport fishermen who can only agree on one thing: banning the other guy's gear.

Fisheries management is a cycle of abuse. Alaska catches fish bound for British Columbia. Fishermen in BC catch fish bound for Washington. People in Washington get fed up with the poor fishing and go up to Alaska for a shot at the fish trying to swim back here.

Fisheries' catch quotas are distributed to the myriad abuser groups through a series of intense negotiations that, judging from the results must involve a whole lot of whiskey and a Ouija board.

What's the poor governor to do but shift the whole mess off to some hired gun director who gets paid to take the heat? The director of our fisheries gets fired so often, we just call him "the new guy." He has a tough job; whatever he does will be wrong.

The new guy can blame the fish and game commission. They are a pack of know-it-all do-gooders, who work for free and set regulations for every species of wild thing that lives in our state, from herring spawn to mountain sheep.

But not even a commission of know-it-alls can know everything. That's why they rely on the expert testimony of bought-and-paid-for biologists and the plundering rhetoric of greed-bloated pressure groups to stack the deck for a self-serving staff of anonymous career opportunists.

No, they don't fish, either. How could they? These poor staff members have spent their entire careers locked up in the basement of the state capitol. The new guy won't let the staff out of the basement until they cough up some more rules, so they do.

All the staff has to work with is a roulette wheel donated by an Indian casino. Every spin of the wheel sets a new season and a new limit somewhere. Research suggests the actual construction of fishing laws is a form of piecework, which would explain why the rulebook gets thicker every year. While I may have skipped a few boilerplate procedural details on the fabrication of our fishing laws, I hope it all makes sense to somebody.

Maybe they should get a new Ouija board.

Tourist Season

Some of the locals have become concerned about the influx of foreigners on the Olympic Peninsula. We should all take a minute to consider that, but for the grace of God, we might all be suffering the same fate as these downtrodden masses. If we understood the trials and tribulations these visitors have endured to get here, we might not be so quick to judge them so harshly.

They are refugees who come to our shores looking for the basic necessities we all take for granted, such as barbecues, coolers full of ice, and an RV dump station. We call them tourists—a stereotype so degrading we even put a season on them. Tourists often appear lost and confused, mostly because they are. But that's still no excuse to take advantage of them, even for money.

During the peak of tourist season, it is possible to count many different species of RVs creeping over hills and squeezing through our narrow historic bridges. Keep a sharp eye out. The back door of a RV can spring open at the oddest times, showering the roadway with personal items, turning a gridlock of tourist traffic and construction delays into a treasure hunt the whole family can enjoy.

Being a tourist is no vacation. Forced to leave one campground in the morning before they are charged for another day, the tourists must find another campground before the evening rush of other campers fills all the spaces. In between, there is scant time to soak up the scenic splendor and find a dump station for the holding tank before there is an accident.

Once you find a place to camp without being arrested, it's then time to set up the RV. This can take hours. Many RV-ers are so addled with creature comforts—the microwave, the hot tub, the skeet range—they have no time to smell the trees, talk to a chipmunk, or notice that someone just stole their firewood.

When you get the RV set up, it's time to relax and meet the neighbors. This can be a good opportunity to look down your nose at those less fortunate than yourself: the tent campers. Efforts to waterproof these crude structures can involve wrapping them in sheets of plastic. Once the campers have set up their leaky tent, the time has come to start the smoky campfire.

How you start a fire in the rain forest is anyone's guess. I watched a tourist light off a creosote-soaked railroad tie for a fire-starter. That old saying about where there's smoke there's fire didn't apply to that particular railroad tie. It just smoked and smoked, treating everyone nearby to a choking fog that could be avoided only by crawling around on the ground. When in Rome …

Others use camping trash to start their fires. By huddling over the garbage fire to heat up a pan of burnt chili, these hardy campers seek to avoid the swarms of biting insects and warm up enough to endure a night in a wet sleeping bag on a leaky air mattress.

As morning arrives, the sounds of the wilderness filter in. Someone has been slamming the restroom door since the birds started singing. A neighbor is splitting the firewood he just stole from your campsite. A pair of rottwielers howl at some kids playing rap music.

The journey through a day in the forest has begun. There's nothing like a fresh cup of hot coffee first thing in the morning when you're camping, even if some mosquitoes and lumps of milk *are* floating on top of it. You'll need plenty of hot coffee to stomach the breakfast of blackened eggs with pork bits.

Doing the dishes on a camping trip can be a disgusting chore. I suggest putting the dishes in a bucket of soapy water, leaving the bucket out in the woods, and switching to paper plates. Those can later be used to start the garbage fire.

Whoever said fish and company smelled after three days never went camping, because as any camper knows, it's entirely possible for people to stink right away. You might suggest your fellow campers go for a swim in one of the many streams, lakes, and rivers on the Olympic Peninsula. Unfortunately, our local waters are cold enough to stop your heart. Our Olympic pioneers didn't start bathing until after the invention of the horse trough, so what makes you think you're tougher than they were? On a typical camping trip, you'll be too busy worrying about wilderness survival to waste time bathing anyway.

You're burning daylight. It's time to move on to another dump station, find another campground, and steal more firewood. It will all be worthwhile when the marshmallows are roasting over the coals.

Olympic Peninsula Retirement Guide

Retirement. The big day finally came. You couldn't believe how lucky you were to retire on the Olympic Peninsula. Just look at those mountains, the forests, and the water! It's a recreational wonderland where you can still go fishing, clamming, and crabbing if you could just find the time. But first things first.

You couldn't wait to buy a view lot and build a retirement dream home that would really wow the relatives. With the price of real estate and construction rising through the roof, you wanted to get started the day before yesterday, but all the big-shot builders were busy.

Besides, getting a building permit around here is like passing a bill though Congress. That's how they justify those outrageous property taxes. Meanwhile, you live like a refugee in an RV, listening to an endless stream of excuses why the builder couldn't finish your house.

All you wanted was a house you could really stretch out in, a couple of stories with a four-car garage and a tower. The neighbor said you were blocking his mountain view. But he didn't know who he was messing with.

The rest of the neighbors were really great. One of them even offered to sell you his fishing boat. You couldn't wait to go fishing. That's all you really wanted to do when you retired—that and just relax after a life in the rat race. But first, you had to finish the dream home and put down a lawn the size of a football field before the rain turned the place into a mud hole.

The realtor said it never rained here, but then he said a lot of things like, "There is no crime."

You knew that was a lie the day after the tweakers moved in next door and began collecting junk cars and dealing drugs to a 'round-the-clock stream of visitors. You worried about getting robbed by the drug addicts. It cost a lot to put in that new burglar alarm system, but it was worth it—until you locked yourself out and tried breaking into your own house.

Your wife said the stress and exhaustion of retirement was affecting your memory. But heck, now that you're stuck together all day without a break, she says all sorts of crazy things, like, "I've always wanted a lavender farm." Who knew?

Between the kids and the job, you haven't had a conversation with the woman in thirty years. You add the lavender farm to the Koi pond, the greenhouse, the vineyard, the orchard, the vegetable garden, the rock garden, and the miniature horses, goats, and llamas to the rest of the honey-do list that's growing faster than the national debt.

You need a lot of tools to do the job right. You had to build a barn that was big enough to fit the tools, the RV, and the boat. Meanwhile, you had to build a fence around your vegetable garden before the deer ate everything. The deer fence worked fine, until the elk walked through it.

You had no idea how much backbreaking labor was involved in retirement. Your back and knees went out from the constant strain of construction, landscaping, and climbing the stairs in your dream home. You found an understanding pharmacy with plenty of pain medications.

You decided to spray the lawn and garden with herbicides, and cover it all with gravel to give it that day-after-the-blast-at-ground-zero look.

By now, you're so stressed out by the endless pressure of retirement, you start to miss that job you hated all those years. You decide to just take off and go fishing. You launch your new boat and cruise way out into the freighter lanes in the middle of the Strait of Juan de Fuca before the engine quits.

Your neighbor must have known! You tow the worthless hull back to your dream home, park it in the front yard and use it as a recycling bin.

Your knees have gotten so bad your ankles start acting up. You buy more pills, more booze, and more herbicide. You spend your days sleeping until noon, then watching TV with a loaded pistol.

And why not? The pain meds have got you so zonked out all you can do is sit in a chair and drool. The new neighbors built a three-story dream house that blocks *your* mountain view.

You're hiding from the constant stream of tweakers knocking on your door looking for the drug house. Every once in a while, you stir from your dream home to venture out to the liquor store, the pharmacy, or the grocery store, where you stagger around the aisles gorging on free samples.

You finally begin to suspect you've lost your mind when you write a letter to the newspaper.

Ain't No Bugs on Me

Someone asked me what was the most dangerous animal on the Olympic Peninsula. Bears? Cougars? Sasquatch? Nope.

The last person to get mauled by a bear around here was a bear hunter. He might very well have had it coming. Some people worry about being attacked by a rogue cougar, but many people have lived here their entire lives and never even *seen* a cougar. Being kidnapped by a Sasquatch isn't likely to happen, either—I've waited for years. She doesn't write, she doesn't call …

The only real danger in the Olympic Mountains are the clouds of stinging, bloodsucking insects you are sure to encounter any time you venture beyond the pavement. Maybe it's just my imagination, or maybe it's global warming—or both. But the bug problem seems to be worse now than at any time in recorded history. Nowadays, bug season starts in January and doesn't stop until late December.

As an expert in wilderness survival, I can tell you how to survive the bugs in our wilderness: stay out of it. If you can't, though, here are a few tips to deal with the bug problem.

Insect repellents are always a good idea. There are many fine brands of bug dope currently on the market, and all are worthless. They're either composed of nerve gas residues or perfumed goop that makes you smell like a pile of bear bait.

No, the best way to repel insects is to take a page from the history books and make your own insect repellent. I used to tie a burning toadstool around my neck. Used since the Middle Ages, the resulting smudge is said to repel insects, vampires, and the devil! The last time I showed up in town wearing a burning toadstool, people acted like I had bad breath or something.

I had to come up with another way of dealing with bugs that didn't offend the prissy types. This process involves curing my hide in a time-honored method employed by mountain men throughout history: I stopped bathing. It can work for you, too.

Once a glaze forms, wipe yourself down with a bacon rind, then apply a thin film of my special-blend lavender bug dope. Composed of equal parts pine tar, creosote, and bathtub lavender oil, my special-blend insect repellent dries into a hard shellac that will break the beak of any mosquito that tries to poke a hole in you.

Side effects may include dizziness, nausea, and chemical pneumonia, but that's nothing compared to spending the night getting eaten alive by mosquitoes. Look on the bright side: you're sure to forget all about the mosquitoes once you're attacked by deer flies. They are like mosquitoes on steroids.

Deer flies can poke a hole in an elk hide, which is tough and hard to cut with a sharp knife. Once a deerfly sets its sights on you, no repellent shy of a .12-gauge shotgun is liable to stop them. The deerfly has the ability to hover and attack from behind when you least suspect it. Chances are you won't notice the deerfly until it's too late, when he's bitten a chunk out of your hide and left a welt you'll scratch for days. I've swatted many a deer fly in the act of sucking my blood only to have them hit the ground and take off for another try.

I've seen people trying to drive the deer flies off each other with tree limbs. This can lead to campers beating each other with chunks of wood even before the booze hits.

It is a little known curious fact that among any party of hikers, there is always at least one unlucky person to whom the bugs seem drawn. This is usually the person who first complains about the bugs.

Once you reach camp, have the designated bug bait sit off a little ways by themselves. Maintain visual contact. Once their eyes swell shut, be sure to check for their wallet.

Still worse than all other bugs put together are the bald-faced hornets and yellow jackets. It's no joke that the allergic reactions to bee stings actually kill more people in the United States every year than poisonous snakes. Home remedies for bee stings include a combination of mud and whiskey applied both internally and externally, neither of which works.

There are some medicines available that can pop the bee's stinger out and relieve the swelling and itching. They belong in every first aid kit. But still, the best advice I can give on how to deal with bugs in the wilderness is to stay out of it.

Trailhead Trash Talk

It is now the law. You now have to carry a trash bag in you car when driving in the State of Washington. This is a story as old a civilization. As soon as early man began gathering into cities, they started passing laws that made no sense to those still living out in the country.

What don't they understand? Out here in the wilderness, the vehicle *is* the litterbag. The terminology of litter itself is an indictment of society's inability to recycle economically. When words like "garbage" or "trash" are tossed around to describe the contents of my vehicle, I feel victimized by the prejudice and ignorance of others. All the contents of my vehicle are essential tools of wilderness survival.

For example, when it's springtime in the Olympic Mountains, people travel here from all over the world to take in the scenic splendor, get lost, or worse.

Maybe you're wondering what could possibly be worse than getting lost in the wilderness? Well, returning to the trailhead after a tough hike and finding your vehicle broken into and all your worldly possessions gone ranks right up around the top.

Go ahead and tell the rangers; they could use a good laugh. You were warned about leaving valuables in a car parked at a federal trailhead. Vehicle break-ins are a popular form of outdoor recreation for certain species of lowlife that infest the hinterlands.

Trailhead thieves have been known to travel from one national park to another, plundering vehicles along the way.

Luckily, there are ways of dealing with these remote break-ins. It's a wilderness survival technique, just one of the many skills every woodsman should know, like the ability to read the signs, hot-wire a car, or siphon gas. Wilderness survival is not just about nature anymore, so you have to grab a bat and ball and get in the game.

I could leave the Hope Diamond on the seat of my truck for a year and no one would touch it. One look at my truck will tell you why; it's the one with the buzzards circling above it. Being a fisherman has its advantages. Sand shrimp, herring, and cured salmon eggs not only make excellent bait for salmon, trout, and steelhead, but are also the fastest rotting materials known to man. I've found that by leaving the old bait containers in the heat of an unopened vehicle, you can create an aromatic force field no crook has the stomach to penetrate.

Of course, there are many other tools available in the crime fighter's arsenal. Garbage itself is another one of our greatest secret weapons against remote vehicle break-ins. Junk food packaging being what it is, it's easier than ever before to trash your car after even a short drive.

If you ever run low on garbage, you can stop most anywhere around here and pick up more. But I doubt you'll have to. And be sure to spread the garbage evenly throughout the interior of your vehicle.

Pay attention now, these final steps are very important. Toss some dirty underwear—men's, of course; this is important!—on top of the garbage, and sprinkle your dash with empty pistol shell casings. Then you can hit the trail secure in the knowledge no one will touch your car with a ten-foot pole.

It is unfortunate that in this day and age, law-abiding citizens are being coerced to confine their garbage in a trash bag instead of putting it where it will do the most good.

Follow these few simple rules to keep your vehicle safe from trail-head thieves. They'll move on to that super-clean SUV with the litter bag, allowing you to enjoy your wilderness experience.

How to Weigh a Fish

Thank you for reading this. Sometimes I think that if you didn't read this, no one would. But you do. You send me the most wonderful cards and letters asking all sorts of crazy questions like, "How do you know how big a fish is if you can't take it out of the water?"

The reader was referring to a law designed to protect the wild steelhead. It requires you to not remove the wild steelhead—which is identified by its intact adipose fin—from the water when you catch and release it.

How you actually measure a large and thrashing wild steelhead without taking it out of the water is a good question. That's where I come in. Weights and measures have always been a sensitive subject for people who catch fish. Sometimes, fish will continue to grow long after they are freezer-burnt.

Measuring a fish without taking it out of the water is an important skill for a fishing guide. I sell dreams of silver fish jumping from bluish-green water. Often, a miserable day of not catching fish in the rain can be transformed into a sport fishing adventure once you realize how big the big one that got away actually was. Using this system, I have routinely hooked several twenty-pound steelhead per day when other boats got skunked. No, we did not actually see many of these fish, mind you. The official weights of these trophies were determined by adding the speed of the current, the arc of the fishing rod, and the blood-alcohol level of the angler.

Just because we didn't actually see or land a trophy steelhead doesn't mean you can't go home with a wall-hanger. Simply determine the exact length and girth measurements of the fish you wished you had caught and one of our many fine taxidermists will be glad to mail you a life-like polyester reproduction of it.

It's when we actually catch a fish—hey, it happens—that the *real* weighing starts. You may not take the fish out of the water. You'll have to "weigh" it with a tape measure. Often by measuring the length and girth of a steelhead, an angler is able to come up with most any weight they want. Allegations that I doctored my own "Guide Model" tape measure to squeeze in an extra inch or two, was nothing more than character assassination from the bass fishermen. There could be many reasons for this.

While the diseased tentacles of the bass fishing cabal rake in the boodle from endorsements, TV, and bass babe calendars, steelheaders help finance this house of cards with an unhealthy dependence on bass lures to catch steelhead. Bass fishermen have always resented this because compared to steelhead, bass are a form or water pollution.

That's the only reason I can think of for someone to accuse me of exaggerating the size of a fish, for money.

Even the most exacting measurements on a wild steelhead in the water in freezing temperatures are subject to various interpretations. Steelhead are like people; they come in all shapes and sizes. Some are sleek, with a high belly fat content. Others are spawned out with slack bellies. Others work out. Measurements conducted on either species will not give you the accurate weight today's catch-and-release sport fishing demands.

Meanwhile, many fish are getting tired of being caught, photographed, and measured. After making it this far through thousands of miles of ocean, filled with other life forms that want to eat them, the steelhead swim back to their home river. They find the mouths of the rivers packed with hungry seals, sea lions, and tribal nets. Then upriver, a fleet of sport fishermen await their return. Once the steelhead survives the catch-and-release process, they still have to swim up into the mountains to spawn.

The future of fishing depends on the fish surviving catch-and-release fishing. Personally, I have too much respect for the wild steelhead as a species to subject it to the tremendous stress of weighing and measuring, or even catching one on some days.

I think it's the least we can do to preserve these magnificent wild fish.

The Dungeness Special

It is daylight on the river, and I'm out to catch a fish. I don't really care what kind. It's been so long since I caught a fish, I've forgotten what they look like. I'm entering fishing withdrawals, and that can make someone with a fishing problem very tense. I thought if I could just catch a fish, even a little one, I could cope with the harsh reality my out-of-control, hollow shell of existence. Right before I punched him, my therapist called it a transference thing.

That's why we're out here at daylight on the Dungeness River in October. It was once the best fishing river in the world. From the high mountain lakes loaded with brook and rainbow trout and land-locked Atlantic salmon, it tumbled down through old-growth canyons full of Spring Chinook, steelhead and Dolly Varden—a char—the size of steelhead. The lower Dungeness had runs of Dog (Chum) and Humpies (Pinks) so thick the farmers used them for fertilizer. There were sea-run cutthroat and even a few sea-run brook trout that had filtered down from the high mountain lakes. The Brookies came back weighing five or six pounds.

Those were the good ol' days when nobody cared if they caught a trout that small. Not when there were steelhead to catch. At one time, the Dungeness was known as the best spring steelhead river in Washington. Being such a fast river, landing a big one was always a problem. You had to be ready to jump in the river and run or swim downstream when the fish took off.

But that was nothing compared to the Spring Chinook fishery. They'd stack up in Dungeness Bay where you could fish them on the tide in the shallow water. The Humpies ran in Dungeness Bay so thick that schools of them would get stranded in the eelgrass at low tide.

These massive runs of fish swam up the Dungeness almost all year-round. Far up into the mountains where they fed people, animals, and birds. They spawned and died, and their carcasses washed back down, fertilizing the river, the forests, and the bay in a life cycle we destroyed before we even understood it. It left us to fish for what we can in the poor Dungeness, a few hatchery-raised silvers. Everything else is either extinct, threatened, or already gone.

As daylight spreads a rosy glow through the river mist, a majestic eagle flies into the dawn. There is the smell of death. A couple of last summer's Humpies, remnants of a run that once numbered in the hundreds of thousands, are laying half out of the water where the snaggers left them. Word that the season has been closed on Humpies for the last forty years in the Dungeness had yet to leak this far upriver.

We notice spoor along the river's edge. Donut boxes, coffee cups, and snoose cans that tell the old guide it's a morning bite in this hole. You've got to be able to read the sign to find the productive water. If there had been a mess of beer cans on the beach, you'd know it was a night fishing hole. This is what we call "matching the hatch."

Often by sifting through the remains of discarded gear packages left on the river's edge, you'll find a secret lure. That's how I discovered a the "Dungeness Special." It's an effective wet-fly pattern retrieved by jerks on the lower river that's super-easy to tie. They just wrap a lead hackle around a big treble hook and tie one on.

But be careful. These days, fishhooks come with a warning label that shows you just how stupid the government thinks you are. It says, "Do not put fish hooks in your mouth." They're right; that's what the donuts are for.

The Dungeness Special is such an incredible lure, fish will bite it with almost any part of their body. Once the tail bite is on, the action can be fast and furious. It's tough to stop at your limit, whatever it may be. Before you know it, the meat fever hits and you have full-metal-jacket combat fishing at its finest.

So it was just my luck that my secret hole was clogged with other fishermen. They all seemed to be using the Dungeness Special. Here, I demonstrated a simple technique to clear the beach without seal bombs or pit bulls. I told the fishermen that the fish cop was headed this way. My fellow anglers took off upstream so quickly, they didn't have a chance to thank me.

Embracing the solitude, I cast into a tree limb on the far shore. The fish have already seen all the fancy casts. If you want action these days, you have to make your lure appear as if it fell out of a tree. How you get a lure that's stuck in a tree limb to fall in the water is your business. It's like they say, 10 percent of the fishermen lose 90 percent of the lures.

My next cast snagged something on the bottom of the river. The seconds ticked by. My lips began to sweat. I set the hook and yelled "Fish on!" My pole bent double until I thought it would break, but it didn't.

"It's a big one!" I yelled. It was a big one—a big tangle of old line, rope, and black plastic. Dragging it across the bottom of the hole released a cloud of mud that turned the river brown.

But a bad day's fishing still beats a good day writing.

Shanghaied!

It was daylight on the water. A heaving deck and the smell of saltwater told me I'd awakened to a real-life nightmare. In the murk of dawn, I could see heavy surf pounding against sheer cliffs that rose into the fog. The morning tide was taking us out into the Pacific past the basalt ramparts of A-Ka-Lat, the Quileute fortress at the mouth of the river that bears their name.

First described by Capt. John Meares in 1788 as a fortified village, A-Ka-Lat was also a burial ground for chiefs and a lookout for spotting whales and enemy raiders. That's how the Quileute saw the Russian brig *St. Nicholas* in 1808. She'd lost her sails in a November gale and wrecked to the south on the rocks of the Quileute Needles.

The Russian captain Nikolia Bulygin of the *St. Nicholas* had orders to build a fort somewhere around the mouth of the Columbia River to counter Spanish, English, and American claims to North America. Instead, the Russians and their Aleut crew were captured and sold as slaves south to the Columbia River and north to the Makah of Cape Flattery.

Of the original crew of twenty—which included Bulygin's wife, Anna Petrovna, the first European woman to live in the State of Washington—seven died in captivity, including Petrovna. The remaining thirteen Russians and Aleuts were rescued in 1810 by Capt. J. Brown of the Boston brig *Lydia*.

If it wasn't for the sharp eyes of the Quileute, we might all be speaking Russian by now.

It wasn't long before we were over the bar of the Quileute River and out into the open sea. Rain was peppering the deck as we made our way through an autumn squall.

Here at the mouth of the Quileute, when they say "rough bar conditions," they aren't referring to the nightlife. The Quileute Bar is a dangerous place even for the U.S. Coast Guard. On February 12, 1997, a rescue lifeboat went down in a fifty-knot wind with thirty-five-foot waves. They were trying to rescue a disabled sailboat to the south near Destruction Island. Three of the four lifeboat crewmen died. One of them was due to be discharged two weeks later.

They don't call it the Graveyard of the Pacific for nothing. And it was just my luck to get shanghaied out in the middle of it.

I'm not the first guy to get shanghaied off the Olympic Peninsula. It's a proud pioneer tradition from Grays Harbor to Port Townsend. It's a hangover from the Age of Exploration when many of the sailors were impressed into service. After the hellish months of vermin infested confinement, floggings, and wormy grub, they found themselves anchored up in a paradise of salmon, clams, and crabs. Jumping ship and living with the Native Americans seemed like a good idea—until the captain paid the natives to hunt you down and bring you back to the ship, where you would be clapped in irons. Some of the guys made it though, and their family names survive here to this day.

With the crew jumping ship to go live with the Indians every time they got near land, what's a sea captain to do but hire on the latest crop of farm boys, loggers, or stray fishermen who came to town most any weekend for a spree.

There a stiff drink and a quick unconscious trip through a trap door was your invitation to a new career at sea aboard a misery ship. It could take years to get back home, if you ever did at all.

I thought that sort of thing had died out years ago. Then I met some shady characters at a boat ramp. They must have slipped something into my cocoa while I was rearranging my tackle box. The next thing I knew, I was headed out to sea with the tuna pirates.

Say what you will about global warming; it's brought the albacore tuna closer to our shore. Lately, they've come within twenty miles.

That's what we heard, anyway, when we headed out to find them. Twenty miles out in the ocean is a long way for anyone in a small boat to attempt, unless you're fishing. Then it's simply a matter of waiting for the right weather and getting a crew together.

Albacore have never been more abundant. Maybe it's just a coincidence, but they are not currently being managed by the State of Washington. Albacore are an international food fish with no season or limit beyond your ethics and food requirements. But you have to find them first.

We ran west of LaPush searching for the warm blue water of the Japanese current that approaches our shore nearer and nearer each summer. LaPush used to be the best salmon fishing hole in Washington. With the miracle of salmon mismanagement and global warming, it has been transformed into tuna town.

We ran west for about four hours and began trolling two jigs on hand lines and two more on rods, and trolled and trolled for hours.

It's peaceful, out of sight of land. The water was calm and blue and warm. Back over the Olympics, we could see pillars of cloud, plumed many thousands of feet high. We basked in a peaceful sun, and were now forty-eight miles from shore.

That seemed like a magic number: the same distance across the Olympics from the Elwha to the Quinault. It was time to turn around.

Something big bit off a 120-pound test leader. There were big, mysterious fins cutting the water. We saw albatross, shearwaters, and a sunfish the size of a pool table. Then we saw tuna!

We had four fish on at once. It was the first quadruple-header of my fishing career! Blood flowed through the scuppers. We hoped the bite would never end, but it eventually did. It was time to head home.

We landed that night back at LaPush with coolers full of meat—chicken of the sea. It was Saturday night in tuna town, and it was good to be alive.

Mars Fishing Update

Recent space exploration has confirmed the presence of a vast sheet of ice on the planet Mars. Normally, I couldn't care less about Mars. To me, traveling to outer space was a complete waste of time. We should be exploring our inner-space, particularly the oceans.

Man has always studied the heavens more than the ocean. Now the oceans are dying off in more ways than we can count. Fish are dying in Hood Canal. There are "dead zones" in the Pacific Ocean just offshore. At Kalalaloch—a place that means "many clams"—there are none. This summer's forecasts predict runs of king and silver salmon through the Strait of Juan de Fuca will be depressed.

The bad news is the Earth is fished out. The good news is that we may soon have other angling options. It's time to move on. Fishermen have always been explorers. The Norse, Irish, and Basque fishermen who discovered America centuries before Christopher Columbus had sense enough to keep their mouths shut and save the best fishing for themselves. So if fishing is done on Earth, it might be time to move on to brave new worlds and fish where no man has fished before.

The discovery of ice on Mars leads to the distinct possibility that there could be water underneath it. Where there is water, there is a chance there could be a fish. Where there is one fish, there could be a run, and we'll want to be ready for some out-of-this-world-class fishing before the rest of the fleet gets launched.

Who knows what we would catch on Mars? The possible effects of intense atmospheric radiation on Martian fish could be anyone's guess. I'm betting there could be some real monsters. After all, no one else has fished it, so far as we know.

I'd go with the heavy gear just to be on the safe side. Run some piano wire on a tuna rod down to a depleted uranium wiggler with a big shark hook on it. Keep a tight line. Give it the old ditch twitch. You shouldn't have to set the hook.

The lack of oxygen could present difficulties to any potential fishermen on Mars. There will be no smoking on Mars. It could be tough to chew snoose in a space helmet. There is no beer on Mars. These are minor details to the serious space fishermen. It will all be worthwhile once you get the hole drilled in the ice and the ice fishing space shack set up.

Of course, if water is eventually discovered on Mars, large sections of the red planet will be designated as fly-fishing only. No fly fisherman is going to want to endure the rigors of space travel to compete on the same water with worm fishermen.

Martian fisheries management options will have to include regulations for the preservation of endangered species. If there are no endangered species on Mars, we'll have to invent some for the preservation of a galactic bureaucracy, which will depend on endangered species for its very survival.

Fishing on Mars might not be for everyone. There have always been those who would ridicule the efforts to push back the boundaries of our knowledge of science or fishing, or the science of fishing. The sad fact is with the way things are going here on Earth, fishing on Mars could soon be the only fishing we've got.

The Ten Commandments of Fishing

I think it was that famous French philosopher, What's His Name, who said, "Hell is other fishermen." With the population of the United States ballooning out of control, there are bound to be more and more fishermen clogging up our rivers in the years to come. All these fishermen have one thing in common: they come to the Olympic Peninsula seeking solitude, only to have that solitude ruined by more and more fishermen chasing fewer and fewer fish.

Scientific experiments have demonstrated that overcrowding is stressful to lab rats, and causes them to engage in anti-social behavior. That goes double for fishermen, which illustrates the need for a modern code of angling ethics: The Ten Commandments of Fishing.

1. Thou Shalt Have No False Fish Gods. There is only one fish God. God. He made the Earth two-thirds water. He made the fish first. The Philistines had Dagon, a half-man, half-fish god. He would have made a great cartoon superhero, but as a Supreme Being? Nah.

2. There Is Only One Captain. Here's a recipe for disaster: take two know-it-alls, place in boat, add water, and shake well. I've seen boats wreck during arguments over "the way." Ask yourself who's running the boat. Then let them.

3. Thou Shall Not Drown: Think of the rest of us. If you drown, some do-gooder will make it illegal. As if we don't have enough fishing laws already …

4. Thou Shall Fish In Vain: You can travel the lengths of the earth, from Siberia to a midnight raid on your neighbor's trout pond, and not catch anything. It happens. We call it "fishing," not "catching."

5. Thou Shall Not Make False Excuses Not Catching Anything. Maybe you had a leaky hip boot or a cranky guide. You didn't catch anything; get over it.

6. Honor The Spawner: The future of fishing depends on fish returning to the creeks to spawn. Once the fish have made it the spawning grounds, leave them alone.

7. Thou Shall Not Steal Thy Neighbor's Water. Neither by pumping it dry or by anchoring on top of it.

8. Thou Shall Not Kill the Fishing: We all do it in our own way. You're reading a book made of trees and water—the same things fish need to survive. We have to share our natural resources with the fish.

9. Thou Shall Not Covet Thy Neighbor's Tackle Box. "Momma always said, life is like my tackle box. We don't know what's in there, but get it outside before it stinks up the whole house!"

10. Give The Water A Rest. It's an old guide trick. When you get a bite, take a break before you make another cast. For everything, there is a season. Let the water rest.

The Fisherman's Prayer Test Fishing Report

I am a fishing guide on the rain forest rivers of the Olympic Peninsula in Washington State. Over the years I've tested many types of fishing gear and techniques in an effort to get an edge to will help me out-fish the competition.

River guiding for salmon and steelhead is an extremely competitive professional sport. You have to consistently produce fish, or your career is over. A guide doesn't just get up one morning and forget how to catch fish. Fishing is like any other sport—you can go into a slump. A fishing slump can put a guide in a tailspin down the slippery slope to depression, poverty, or even worse—a real job. We hear about this sort of personal tragedy on the river every year. A guide hocks his boat and gets a job. Their names are never mentioned on the river again.

People think it's easy to catch fish and get paid for it. The truth is, it's often harder to catch fish when there's money involved. There could be many reasons for this. When you go fishing with your buddies, they generally know how to fish, or at least how to stay out of the way. New clients can require an extensive break-in period. I used to explain the basics of fishing out of a drift boat in a big hurry to new clients in the predawn darkness while I launched.

"Rushing the client" is a hazing ritual designed to break the angler's spirit by convincing them they're late. This shifts the blame for a bad day's fishing from the guide and back to the clients, where it belongs. Then it's "the client's fault" if they don't catch a fish, because they were "late."

Once the clients are convinced they are too late to catch a fish, that's no excuse not to keep hurrying. The constant rushing is the guide's best defense against the No. 1 job hazard we face: questions.

"How deep is the river?" "Are we sinking?" "How will I know if I hook a fish?"

"You'll know," I explain. "That's when the screaming starts! Until then, you can give your heart to Jesus, but your carcass belongs in the seat of that drift boat!"

Sitting in a drift boat seat may not seem like a big deal, but it is. The chairs are positioned to keep the human cargo balanced. Without balance, I cannot row through the rapids. If I can't row, I can't steer, and we are all going to die.

Usually the client would jump at the chance to hop in the boat. Especially if they've just spent the last hour watching the boat in the dark, shivering from the cold and the fear of what I said was about to pull up dragging a drift boat.

"Watching the boat" was another client-hazing ritual I would use to get an edge on the competition. That's where one or the other prospective clients stayed with the boat while we shuttled my rig downriver to the take-out. This could take hours if we stopped for donuts or did some road hunting on the way. Prospective clients often couldn't be trusted alone at a boat launch. They could blab sensitive information to other fishing guides, who routinely conduct a form of industrial espionage under the guise of polite conversation. But not when I got done with them.

Take my word for it. After watching the boat, prospective clients will hurry aboard to get near the heater and away from the gang of illegal immigrant, sex-offender war criminals that just showed up at the launch dragging their drift boats behind them.

I know it was wrong to say those things about the other fishing guides. Some of it was even untrue. The illegal aliens may be taking a lot of jobs Americans no longer want, but guiding isn't one of them. Fishing guides are like unorganized galley slaves rowing monstrous loads of humanity down wild rivers in search of some of the rarest fish that swim. Maybe we play a little rough, but that's what it takes to get an edge on the competition and put fish in the boat. Or so I thought.

You need more than a boat to catch fish. You need patience and faith in your gear. The greater your faith, the more patience you'll have. The more patience you have, the more fish you'll catch. But it's hard to have patience when you're not catching fish. That's when you can reach a crisis in faith that can cause you to feel lost. Sometimes when you are lost, it's best to figure out how you got there.

I was basically a nice person until I got into a boat. Once aboard, I did a lot of things I'm not very proud of. I used manure worms for bait. I stacked the deck in a steelhead derby by picking up stray bank maggots—aka, shore fishermen—so I'd have more rods in the boat. I won that steelhead derby by stuffing rocks in a fish. That was just an average day on river. Multiply that by a life spent on the water, and I'd become the kind of person I didn't like very much. I started not catching fish even when there were no clients to blame. It wasn't working for me.

At one point, I had been skunked so many days in a row, fishing had become like a *job*. Sure, it's fun to joke around about a guy getting a job. But not when the joke's on me.

I knew I knew I needed help. I was so desperate for a hook up, I begged God for a fish.

I remember it like it was yesterday. I was fishing the Hoh River and couldn't get a bite. I knew there were king salmon around; I could see them rolling on the surface of the water. I anchored up at the head of the hole and let go with a cut plug herring and The Fisherman's Prayer. I barely got the words out of my mouth and it was "fish on!" It was a big king, about forty pounds or so. Then we caught a big silver (Coho) salmon, about eighteen pounds. Then we caught a steelhead, and big bull trout and a sea-run cutthroat. We had caught what every angler on the Olympic Peninsula lays awake nights dreaming about:

the grand slam of the Hoh River! All caught in one day with The Fisherman's Prayer!

Later that season, I was anchored up in the Three Rivers hole, where the Sol Duc and Bogachiel River come together to form the Quileute. The silver salmon were jumping everywhere. There must have been a hundred guys lined up casting every known lure at them. But no one caught a thing.

Silvers are like that. Some days they'd rather jump and splash than bite a lure. It's almost like they don't want to die or something.

That was until The Fisherman's Prayer. Then it was "fish on!" And on and on and on! Using The Fisherman's Prayer increased my catch rate so much, I was able to relax and actually enjoy fishing again. My clients thought I'd gone soft or something, but they didn't care. They were too busy catching fish to notice that I'd stopped yelling at them.

The Fisherman's Prayer belongs in every tackle box. It's based upon the time-tested formula of the Lord's Prayer, given to us by Jesus almost 2,000 years ago. Fishing has gotten a whole lot worse since Jesus. The Fisherman's Prayer has been specifically reformulated for today's tough fishing conditions. The Fisherman's Prayer is legal even in catch-and-release waters that require artificial lures with barbless hooks. Using bait with The Fisherman's Prayer almost isn't fair. From the deep sea to the high alpine lakes, The Fisherman's Prayer works on all species of salt and freshwater game fish. Don't go fishing without a prayer.

1. Fisherman's Prayer

The Fisherman's Prayer

Our Father, above the water, hallowed be thy name.
Thy rain will come. Thy rivers run on Earth
as they do in heaven. Give us this day our daily fish and
forgive our excess limit.
As we forgive those who set the limit.
Lead us not into rough water.
Deliver us at the end of season.
For thine is the river and the ocean and the glory.
Forever and ever. Amen.

2. Fisherman's Serenity Prayer

Fisherman's Serenity Prayer

God, grant me the serenity to accept there are
fish I cannot catch …
the courage to catch the fish I can …
and the wisdom to know the difference.

3. 23 ½ Psalm.

23 ½ Psalm

The Lord is my guide. I'm limited out.
We float the green rivers.
Down the waters of peace.

Though I row through the rapids of the canyons of death,
I don't fear drowning. For you are with me.

Good fishing will follow me all the days of my life.
And I will dwell on the rivers of the Lord.
My whole life long.

4. I wanted to catch every fish in those mountains.

5. You want to be there when the ice is off.

6. Be careful not to remove the fish from the water.

7. The Spruce stump was a wall for my camp

8. He started hanging around that stretch of river.

9. Hoh River Chinook Salmon caught on Fisherman's Prayer.

10. Mountain trout caught on Fisherman's Prayer.

11. Spring Chinook caught on Fisherman's Prayer.

12. Creek fishing with Fisherman's Prayer.

13. Our Father above the water hallowed be thy name

14. They rain will come.

15. They Rivers Run.

16. On earth as they do in heaven.

17. Give Use This Day our daily fish and forgive our excess limit.

18. As We Forgive those who set the limit.

19. Lead us not into rough water.

20. Deliver us at the end of season.

21. Yours is the river ocean and the glory forever and ever amen.

22. The water filled the river.

The water filled the river
The river shaped the land
The land has been forever
The history of man.

23. Shadowed in the timber.

Shadowed in the timber
The river voices flow
And cause me to remember
A hundred years ago.

24. Upriver.

Upriver

Looking upriver that December day, I had to
Squint in such a way.
To stare into the solstice light, that turned
The water silver white.
And looking downriver from where I came
Lay an abysmal canyon the light disdained.
Astride the border, where light and dark meet,
I could see only what lay at my feet.
Blind to the future, forgetting the past,
I could but hope this peace would last.

25. River Bird.

River Bird

I saw a river bird out on a mighty stream.
Her call was barely heard, a whisper in a dream.
Enjoying this as all her days, fluttering
Through a tortured maze
Of white water pounding statues of black rock.
Being near to drowning, I was transfixed in shock.
That such a frail and feathered thing
Should live a life of ease,
In such tumultuous surroundings,
Is encouraging to me.

River Birds

Maybe I'm not the best one to write about river birds. As a fishing guide, we're in direct competition with them for fish. In the spring, there is a downstream migration of baby salmon and steelhead, out of the mountains to the sea. That's only if they can make it through the flocks of fish ducks, fish hawks, herons, kingfishers, and herons. They all gather at the river to breed and gorge on the easy pickings.

The male mergansers are brightly colored with iridescent green heads. The females are a mottled brown. Once the breeding season is over, the males head back out to sea to take care of their feathers. The females are left to raise a brood of chicks on a river where everything wants to eat them.

Baby mergansers start out as downy little puffballs. They ride on their mother's back if there's room. She can have a dozen chicks or more. I saw one merganser with twenty-one babies.

On a diet of straight fish, they are soon too big to ride on their mother's back. The chicks follow her upstream with a flightless paddle-kick, which shoots out a little rooster tail. Once something spooks them, a family of runaway fish ducks looks like a pack of miniature jet skis headed upriver. Or they'll dive and scatter downstream to hide under a logjam.

Once the baby fish ducks learn to fly, the real fishing starts. It's a complex interplay that's painful for a fisherman to watch.

The mergansers fly upstream in the morning and land in a line spread out across the river. Swimming with the sun at their backs, they dip their heads beneath the surface looking for fish.

A pair of dippers twitter endlessly back and forth across the river. The dipper, or water ouzel, is a small, drab gray bird about the size of a sparrow with the unique ability to walk underwater. The rest of the time they stand on rocks twittering, bobbing up and down like they're having a seizure.

An eagle lands on a limb. We don't call them the bald-headed buzzard for nothing. They'll eat anything from a fish duck to a spawned-out salmon. The eagle sits in the tree, trying to make up its mind.

A flock of crows flies in to hassle the eagle. More land on the beach and complain about the fishing.

The fish ducks keep swimming upstream where a bird that looks like a long legged pterodactyl is landing at the head of the hole. The great blue heron can choke down a trophy trout whole or cut it up with his scissors-bill and gulp it down in chunks. He stands in the shallows, waiting.

A pair of belted kingfishers swoops out of the trees. The call of the kingfisher sounds like someone shaking a can full of rocks. With a beak too big for its head and a head too big for its body, the kingfisher defies the laws of physics by hovering over the water just ahead of the fish ducks. They stop and watch the kingfisher dive.

He comes up with a fish, lifts out of the water, and flies back into the trees with his mate. That's a sign for the fish ducks to dive, swimming upstream like feathered torpedoes. The heron wades deeper. The fish are caught in a fish-duck vice.

I step out of the trees and ruin it for everyone. The heron flies away with some indignant squawks. The fish ducks bob to the surface choking down fish. They panic and take off downriver with their bellies dragging the water.

The eagle is still there, sitting on a limb at the tail-out. He watches me hook a steelhead and wrestle it onto the beach. I gut the fish; the heart was still beating. I throw it in the river and leave the rest of the guts on the beach.

The eagle watches, shifting his weight from one foot to the other. He's waiting for me to leave. So I do.

River Monkey

There are strange sights to be seen on the Hoh River in winter.

"I saw a monkey sitting on a log," my fancy friend said one day as we floated through the Rain Forest.

"Was it a big monkey?" I asked.

"A very big monkey!" he said.

"That's just Harvey the brush ape. He doesn't mean any harm" I lied. There was no time to explain to the poor person sitting in the front of the boat that we had to get out of there before something bad happened, again. We were in mortal danger of being casualties of a primate behavior research project gone berserk.

Bigfoot, or Sasquatch—also known as Stick Indians, Skookum, or Seatco—are part of a tradition of large hairy ape-like creature that has haunted this land since before the beginning. Every tribe on the Olympic Peninsula has an oral tradition of these creatures.

They tell of a village wiped out by Skookums on Hood Canal. And of a war above what is now Blyn on Sequim Bay with a cannibal ogress that was stealing children. There was a battle between the S'Klallam and the Quileute when the giant buried them under a landslide to form Lake Crescent. A gathering of Quinault, Cowlitz, and Chehalis were wiped out at Enchanted Valley up the South Fork of the Quinault River. The same thing was supposed to have happened up the Wynoochee River.

The Press Expedition spent the winter of 1890 lost up the Elwha River. They had been warned of Seatco by Washington's former territorial governor, Eugene Semple. Seatco had a bad reputation for causing landslides and knocking over giant trees with a stick. That's how they got the name "Stick Indians."

The Press Expedition met a party of S'Klallam hunters up the Elwha valley near what is now the Olympic National Park boundary. The hunters told the explorers they had no idea what was upstream. Of course, this might have just been a S'Klallam story to keep the hunting and fishing for themselves. Their traditions say the Sasquatch had their own territory where the S'Klallam did not go.

In 1924, S'Klallam journalist George Totsgi wrote in the *Olympic Tribune*, a Port Angeles newspaper, on July 18, 1924: "Indians would not go up the Elwha River without many white men along because of their fear of the Stick Siwashes."

History records another example of the Native American dread of what lurked in the rugged, unknown interior of the Olympic Mountains. In July 1885, Lt. Joseph P. O'Neil hired an "old Indian guide" for his U.S. Army expedition south of Port Angeles. That was until the guide found out where they were going—up Ennis Creek.

O'Neil describes how no amount of pay or death threats would detain the guide once he saw where the expedition was camped and where they were going; the guide ran out of camp the first night. O'Neil chalked it up to a native superstition, a fear of the Thunder Bird—the mythical monster bird large enough to catch whales, said to nest in the Olympics. But it might have been something else.

Maybe it was just a coincidence, but O'Neil also mentions a lot of screaming at night around their camp. The mules were stampeded into the timber. This camp was on Skull Creek, a small tributary of Ennis Creek, named for the discovery of a well-preserved human skull the expedition turned up while cutting a trial.

Native Americans did travel up into the interior of the high Olympics, and the Stick Indians obviously didn't kill everyone who went upriver.

Boston Charley, the S'Klallam hunter, told of breaking his leg in the headwaters of the Elwha and being cared for by a Sasquatch who brought him berries and water. Maybe it was the same Stick Indian that followed him home one autumn down at the mouth of the river and took all of the fish out of his smokehouse and left a calf elk in trade.

Many people have seen the Sasquatch since then. Many more have heard calls and screaming around their camps in the woods at night. That's normal in these hills. You should have heard the scary noises at night around camp once *my* hunt for Bigfoot started.

The terrifying scream of the Sasquatch seemed tame compared to the chest beating, posturing, and eating noises emanating from the nightly buffet.

I'd be the first to admit, I was only in the hunt for Bigfoot for the money and possible future product endorsements. I could'a been a contender. A lot of folks claimed to be hunting Bigfoot, but I had Bigfoot hunting me. He was always hanging around, knocking over coolers and raiding the garbage can. He liked to push trees over just for fun. Or sometimes just stand there and watch me chop wood. You always knew when he was around when you heard the calls of ravens and other birds that were too loud to come from a bird.

You generally see a raven when he calls. They want the world to look up and take notice. Anything that doesn't is liable to be the raven's next meal. The fact is, some bird calls in the woods weren't made by birds at all. Harvey was a mimic who could sound like anything from a bugling bull elk to a police siren. He liked to scream around the camp at night when he ran out of beer.

That was a mistake, leaving bowls of beer on the riverbank at night. I thought I could lure the creature in and get him drunk enough for a quick ride to the zoo. But alas, it was merely another failed experiment in primate research.

For whatever reason, I failed to acquire funding for my hunt for Bigfoot. I had to cut costs; expenses were mounting. Accidents will happen. Like when the plaster of paris—used to make impressions of the creature's track—was dumped into the pancake batter. Or when alcohol intended to preserve stool samples was dumped into the punch.

Then, a series of large footprints were found in the mud. It looked like a human foot, except for the fact that it was large enough for my size twelve boot to fit inside with room to spare. This called for expert analysis. I called Professor Grover S. Krantz, an anthropology professor who had retired in Sequim. Professor Krantz was the "Father of Cryptozoology," the study of undiscovered animals. Dr. Krantz had never seen a Sasquatch himself, but he thought they existed based upon the physical evidence he had examined: their tracks, hair, dung, and a fossil record that stretched back a million years or so.

He made a cast of the track. Then, based on a series of measurements he would not reveal, declared the track a fake. I guessed that meant he wouldn't want any of the dung sample collection, either.

This created a more terrifying possibility. The prospect of a large hairy ape stalking the camp was one thing, but the idea of some idiot walking around barefoot in the middle of hunting season when the woods were full of hunters shooting at anything that moved 24-7 … now that was *really* scary. The hunt for Bigfoot sort of fizzled after that. It was okay.

Dr. Krantz wanted to collect a specimen of this undiscovered ape species to prove it really existed. That's what got me wondering who the real savage beast was. Except for knocking over a few trees and throwing some rocks, Harvey had never done anything to get shot over. Meanwhile, the human race had plundered the natural resources of this land into economic extinction in just a few short years.

I told Harvey he was lucky, he was a fake and a fraud, and didn't exist. He'd stay that way if he knew what was good for him. Many creatures, from the hundred-pound salmon to the Olympic Mountain Moonshiner, have gone extinct shortly after they were discovered.

Harvey just moped around the woods near the camp, moaning. I cut off his beer ration. He'd yell "Hey!" once in a while, like he was ordering another round. I could tell he was depressed, but I had my own problems. Once you discover Bigfoot, how do you get rid of him?

I thought he was one of those problems you could ignore and they would just go away.

The fall salmon had started running. The eagles moved upriver to hunt the salmon. The bald eagle is the fishermen's best friend. Eagles sit in the trees and watch the fish. Once you figure out the eagles, it's like having your own private bird dog for fish. I thought it was only fair if the eagles were going to "bird dog" the fish, I'd feed them the heads and guts. I started cleaning the fish at the same spot along the river. Some days, the eagles seemed to be waiting for us, and on other days, they weren't. I threw the fish heads and guts on the same stretch of beach anyway. I figured the eagles would get them eventually. But I was wrong.

Harvey started hanging around that stretch of beach. You could tell from the smell of a dead billy goat, and there were no more eagles or any other birds on the gut pile. We heard a raven calling from back in the woods, but we never saw it.

"That sure is a loud raven," my fancy friend said.

"It sure is," I lied, rowing downriver as hard as I could.

We hadn't caught anything that day. Fishing is like that. Some days, the only sure way to get a fish is to go to a supermarket. Harvey did not understand this concept of not catching fish. It was my fault; I had violated the prime directive of wilderness travel. I had fed the wildlife. I had become Harvey's supermarket, and now the supermarket shelves were bare. Harvey registered his displeasure.

When were kids, we used to play "Sink the Navy." That was a game where we threw a stick in the river and threw rocks at it. Whoever hit the stick "sunk the navy."

Before I knew it, Harvey was trying to sink my navy.

"Kersploosh!" a big rock sailed out of the woods and landed with a splash only five feet off our stern.

"What was that?" my fancy friend asked.

"A fish jumped!" I lied.

"Why don't we try to catch it?" he asked.

"Oh, it was just an old spawner," I replied, lying again and launching into a guide yarn about how no real sportsman would try to catch fish off their spawning bed.

"Yes I would!" My fancy friend said. "I'd like to catch … something"

"Let's go downstream. This hole has a lot of snags." I said, continuing my untruthful roll. He made a cast anyway, and—wouldn't you know it?—caught a big bright steelhead. He wanted to catch another, but it was starting to get dark.

I cleaned the fish, threw the guts on the beach. It was way past time to get out of there.

Judgment

I

They say madness drove him to this place.
Where snow falls from the rocky face.
Beware what stalks this wretched waste.
Ye that pass with fear in haste.
The bones that lie upon the trace
Testify the fate of race.

The moon is rising on the moor.
The hound doth bound upon the spoor.
The master's shot has struck the fore
To drive the beast in hell's backdoor.
Master and hound heard never more.
Their remains the added score.

The sleeper falls into a trance
In the hills where devils dance.
With ancient pagan ritual
They prepare their victual.

Who remembers the bloody spot.
As well to ask the wife of Lot.
They say of God, he knows not.
He is thus bereft of thought.

With no mind to be out of.
Ill deserving human love.
His speech but shrieks of confusion,
Perhaps it is man's illusion.

Of blind men touching things unseen.
The cleric and the physic's scheme
The propensity to explain
What we rule in our domain.
That we cannot subjugate
Bears the malice of our hate.

II

They say madness drove him to this place.
Far from the faithless human race.
By day, he lies in a vale of green.
By night, he walks where no man's been.
To gather herbs on which he feeds.

He worries not of future needs.
He gathers no treasure upon this earth.
All share equal at his hearth.
Seeing all while he is unseen.
From yonder hills where he does reign.

Yet not the least of his ability
Is his oracular facility.
The prophecy of lunacy
Bears ironic destiny.

As was writ in sacred verse,
They that are last shall be the first.
They who sit on Earth's high thrones.
Accursed to gnaw upon the stones.

The Last Fish of Summer

It is daylight on the river. Fall is on the way. You can tell by the way the leaves are changing colors and falling faster as the days pass. The morning's socked in with fog so thick it drips.

We launch on the river in the dark and float in the vapors. Even the fish ducks are lost in the gloaming. They fly past our heads at eye-level, just swerving to miss us. The river drops sharply over some big rocks. In the dim light, it's like floating off the edge of the known world.

There is the sound of rocks clattering ahead—that must have been what spooked the fish ducks, indistinct shapes moving in the fog. We stop to witness one of the greatest spectacle events in nature, two big bull elk with huge trophy racks locked in brutal combat right in front of us.

We stop and stare in wide-mouthed wonder as these two monsters beat their heads together with a cracking sound as their antlers connect.

This is no posturing display. The bulls can lose an eye, break something, or suffer a bad puncture from the raking they give each other. I once found two dead five-point bull elk whose antlers had locked together on impact.

That must have been a tough way to go, starving to death with a mortal enemy stuck to your head like a hyperactive Siamese curse. Maybe the cougars got to them first. Either way, these poor bulls were skeletons by the time I came upon them.

The elk on shore appeared to be unevenly matched, one bull much larger than the other. For some reason, the smaller bull was doing all of the shoving. He had the big old bull down on his hindquarters in the river. They broke apart then circled around on shore for a while before whacking their heads together again. There was some heavy breathing.

A cow elk waded across the river. She stepped onto the far shore and sauntered past the bulls as if they didn't exist. The bulls stopped fighting and followed her, single file, over logs, like a vertical steeplechase up the side of the hill.

Then the gravel bar went silent. It took a while to remember we're fishing the elusive summer-run steelhead. They are called the fish of a thousand casts, or 10,000 oar stokes. But who's counting?. Sometimes, it's best not to keep score or nurse grudges where fishing is concerned.

You just have to accept the hard fact that as tough as the summer-run steelhead is to hook, they're even more difficult to land. In summer, the water temperature is warmer. That could make a fish more active. I don't know. But they like to swim straight at you, and that puts a lot of slack in the line if you don't reel it in fast. A slack line will make many fishermen give up and quit, when all of a sudden, the fish will fly into the air, jumping around with a hook in its mouth.

With some luck, it's still on the end of your line.

I once had a steelhead rush the boat and jump eye-level, right at the edge of the boat. There was no slack. I nosed the fish over so it landed in the boat on top of an open tackle box. Then the real battle began. If you think a steelhead is hard to land, try grabbing a live one in the bottom of a boat.

On a good day, you can catch a summer steelhead. On a great day, you can get your limit. All eyes are on you back at the fish camp where the fish cleaning ritual unfolds. That's where all the fishermen gather to see who caught what. There are those that are just too nosy for their own good.

You know the type. They just can't seem to mind their own business, no matter where they are. They can't just leave a poor fisherman to clean his fish in peace. No, this pest waddles across the rocks, wagging his fat belly and staring at me from behind that ridiculous walrus-looking mustache.

He is the Termin-Otter, the largest river otter on the Olympic Peninsula. He doesn't even bother fishing anymore. He's got me trained to feed him the fish guts and heads. He stashes them for later in a little cave across the river. It's all part of a fishing feud that goes a long way back to the good old days, when fishing was all that really mattered. Back when we stalked the high mountain lakes to be there just as the ice was off. That could be the best fishing of the year. You almost didn't have to pack food in. You could live on trout, if you caught some.

I'll never forget the year I was early for ice-out. The Fourth of July found me hip deep in the snow on a still-frozen lake. Except for a pool at the outlet the size of a truck bed, the lake was still covered with a couple of feet of ice.

The outlet was so jammed with driftwood, it was impossible to fish—or so I thought.

There, thousands of feet above the Elwha River, an otter came bounding across the snow. You don't think of otters as land animals, but they are. Otters can run as fast as a dog. This one was a mountain climber. It ran to the outlet of the frozen lake and dove into that tiny patch of open water. I've tried to hold my breath as long as an otter can stay under water, but I can't. Just when I thought the otter had drowned, he popped up to the surface with a four-pound brook trout wagging in his mouth.

I had a lump of butter and little else but some instant mashed potatoes in my pack. I could smell the trout simmering in the butter. Out of my head with hunger, I waited until the otter was on shore and rushed him. I thought the otter would get scared and drop the fish. Obviously, I didn't know otters.

The otter didn't move. He just waited until I got close and started growling. That stopped me in my tracks. The otter dove back in the lake, and I never saw it again. Maybe the otter drowned trying to get away with his fish, but I doubt it. Otters are about the toughest animal there is. He must have had some air holes in that lake somewhere. I walked back to camp feeling like a savage. I've been throwing fish guts to the otters ever since.

The otters are extra fat this year. It is going to be a hard winter.

Alien Fish Camp

And so, another salmon season passes dead astern. I hope you did better than I did, huddled by the stove, trying to dry out a soaked hide—mine. Waiting for the landfill to open so I can dump what's left of a woodsman's kit thirty years in the making, before one more so-called fishing buddy drops by to observe: "You sure know how to build a campfire … ha, ha."

Tent camping in the monsoon season of the Olympic Peninsula rain forest can be a thrilling nature experience. When the wind hits the old-growth timber, bad things start falling out of the sky. Treetops bigger than a telephone pole can bust off and plow into the forest floor like a giant spear. Slabs of loose bark and broken limbs can fly hundreds of yards through the air in the wind. Or the whole tree, along with a bunch of its neighbors, can simply blow over.

With wind comes the rain. A tropical Pacific rain can blow in and melt the new snow for many thousands of feet up the mountains. The creeks become rivers, and the rivers become war zones of big trees plowing their way downstream like a big wood highway.

This can happen so fast, you can wake up in the river if you don't watch where you camp. Lying awake all night listening to the roar of the rising river and the frightening crash of big timber hitting the ground is enough to make you wish for an abduction by aliens.

But we camp in the monsoons anyway. The salmon run upstream on the high water. You want to be on the river in the fall when the river is dropping and clearing from mud brown to emerald green.

I drove up the Hoh River Valley looking for a place to camp. Any given day on the Hoh River in the fall can be the best fishing there is. I drove to the end of an old grade and walked out a short way to look at the river.

A bald eagle sat in a snag at the head of a long, slow drift, staring down between his feet. A king salmon rolled like a small torpedo half out of the river.

When the kings run upriver in the fall, the rest of the fish—the Coho, steelhead, and sea-run cutthroat—run with them. We just call them all bluebacks to avoid confusion.

I figured that if I set up my tent quickly, I could catch a nice salmon before dark. I went to work in a patch of small trees, lashing together the classic fish camp with all the trimmings.

Nothing beats a bough bed for comfort in the wilderness. Constructed properly, a bough bed is sturdy yet springy, and it smells terrific.

Next to sleeping, eating seems to be the next-most-popular camp activity. It helps to have a well-organized folding camp kitchen. There are many fine ones on the market. I found a wire rope spool sitting in the landing of an old logging show, set a gas stove and some boxes on top, and that was the kitchen.

Once you rig the camp kitchen, you'll want to begin work on the restroom facilities. Latrine placement is crucial on a dark and stormy night. Your facilities should be waterproof, with a door snug enough to keep the skunks out. They don't like to be surprised.

I camped in a grove of second-growth timber. Within the grove was the dark hulk of a monolithic stump more than a dozen feet high and at least eight feet in diameter—all that was left of a tree more than 200 feet tall. It might have been about 500 years old.

The Olympic Peninsula rain forest grows the biggest spruce in the world. Spruce was used for building airplanes back in World War I. Only the best trees with clear wood and straight grain were used.

That was hand logging at it's finest. The loggers climbed the up the massive spruce by standing on spring-boards, planks set in notches chipped in the side of the tree. They might have had to climb above the butt swell, where it would be easier to cut the giant down with nothing but an ax and a crosscut saw. There's a lot of pitch in a big spruce stump. The old loggers packed kerosene to keep the saw from gumming up in the cut while they were sawing.

It must have been quite a sight to watch the big spruce go over. The cutters would have been ten feet up the stump when the tree started falling. Once they got the tree on the ground, the real work started. They bucked the logs to length and split them into beams, called "cants," with wedges pounded by a heavy log sledge suspended on a tripod.

They wrestled the cants to the river and floated them down to the mouth, where some captain courageous boomed them out through the surf of the open Pacific Ocean—all for the war effort.

That old spruce stump was more than just a historic monument. It was a perfect back wall for my camp. I rigged a pole from the tent to the stump and lashed on a tarp.

By the time I got things set up, it was too dark to fish. I heard splashing down at the river. It might have been the salmon jumping or elk crossing the river. Whatever it was, I was camped in the right spot. It stopped raining.

The stars came out so I started a small campfire and sat out to watch them. Building a campfire in a soggy November in the Hoh rain forest is no easy job. As soon a piece of dead wood hits the ground, it soaks up enough water to start growing moss and sprouting mushrooms.

Your only chance of building a fire in these woods is to find some dry pitch or bring along some fire starter.

I had thought of everything in this camp, even dry cedar kindling from home. I sat and listened to the river and stared into the flames. For a moment, there was a feeling of such peace and contentment, to be in a snug camp, in country loaded with fish and game.

Then a small root attached to the massive spruce stump caught fire. I thought that was a handy bit of good luck. It would save on the firewood packing. I built up the fire to a cheery blaze.

As the flames climbed higher, the surface of the stump appeared moist. I thought it was wet from the rain, but I was wrong. The moisture was melting pitch running down the stump. The big spruce must have been cut in the spring when the sap was running. Once the tree was cut, the sap coagulated in the stump until it fossilized. I now know there must have been enough pitch in that stump to fill a dump truck.

Suddenly, the melted pitch caught on fire. In just a few minutes, the entire stump erupted into a wall of flames. It showered my tent with a blizzard of red-hot cinders.

I grabbed an ax and started chopping poles and slashing ropes, trying to rip my camp apart before it burned down. The flames leaped higher.

In no time, the stump looked like a rocket stuck in the ground. Little trees burst into flames. The moss was catching on fire. I ran around, beating out flames with a shovel.

Daylight revealed a scene of awesome devastation. There was a smoking crater where the Spruce stump had been, and a melted outhouse. Some nosy road hunters stopped by and wanted to know what happened.

"There is only one explanation," I said. "Alien abduction."

Fishing in Winter

There is something magical about fishing winter, when the snow falls down in a curtain of white and makes the river look almost black. You hook a steelhead and watch it bust from the surface of the water and fly up into the falling snow on the end of your line, and know you've seen what few others have. Most people have more sense than to fish in a blizzard.

Fishing in the snow is a good way to escape the crowds. You should always tell someone where you're going on your winter camping trip and when you'll be coming back, unless you're fishing. In that case, the less said, the better; you don't want people finding your secret fishing hole.

It's a good idea to get an early start on any winter fishing expedition, unless you can't. It was after noon by the time I drove to the end of the road up the South Fork of the Hoh River. Near white-out conditions told me the prospect of being snowed in was excellent. No one in their right mind would be fishing in a storm like this, so there was a good chance I'd have the river all to myself.

I took off upriver for the solitude of the big trees. Walking through the silent columns of the old growth in a blizzard of platter-sized snowflakes was a hypnotizing experience. That was my excuse, anyway, for losing the trail. I got hypnotized and turned around in a swamp full of old-growth devil's club. They are like a rain forest cactus growing in clumps of thorny canes. Touching a devil's club can set the whole mess into a springy snake-like motion that leaves you with a lot of thorny, painful souvenirs.

It's at times like these we question the wisdom of winter camping. It was getting dark. I didn't know what time it was, since my watch and everything else I had on was soaking wet by then. I wallowed out of the frozen swamp and tried to find the river. After a while, I came to a grove of big firs above a nice fishing hole. I had to build a fire.

We used to say out in the woods that a man's best friend is a good sharp ax. It was, until I broke its handle off, leaving me with nothing but a dull head to chop some dry kindling out of a frozen wilderness. That's when I remembered I forgot to bring some fire starter from home.

It's hard to pack enough fire starter to burn wood so wet it has mushrooms growing out of it. I've tried it all, from highway flares to pieces of my hip boots. But the best fire starter is the stuff you don't have to pack: pitch.

To build a fire, you need enough pitch to set the mushrooms ablaze. Pitch is where you find it. The old-growth fir and spruce will get a hole in their bark from a bear or other trees hitting it. Pitch will flow from the wound by the gallon. Sometimes you can find lumps of near-fossilized pitch on the forest floor, or you can look into the massive hollow trunk of a windfall.

Pitch is buried treasure. It can be the difference between having hypothermia and a barbecue. But you have to find it first. I felt very fortunate that day to find an old fir about eight feet in diameter that had blown down across a little gully.

There was a wheelbarrow load of pitch in the stump, and the bark was loose. I pried off some bark slabs the size of a truck bed and about ten inches thick. Old-growth fir bark burns like coal once you get it going.

By then, the snow was knee-deep. I built a bark platform on top of the snow and lit off a pitch bomb. I covered the burning pitch with bark slabs. A pillar of thick gray smoke rose through the snowy gloom of twilight. I made a lean-to out of a plastic sheet in a hollow beneath a big fir that must have been eight to ten feet through. It was a cozy den that reflected the heat of the fire.

I drug in a truckload of bark for night wood and watched the blizzard melt in the fire. I cooked a pot of sludge for dinner and lay down to watch the snow falling in the firelight.

I must have gone to sleep, because I remember waking up. It had stopped snowing. The fire had melted a big crater in the snow, but it was burning low. I threw on some more bark and pitch and soon had the fire roaring again.

I heard a noise like thunder or a passing jet aircraft rumbling through the hills in the dark. The snow was melting from the tops of the trees. Lumps of snow, tree limbs, and tops were falling out of the old-growth canopy.

For whatever reason, I built up the fire some more. This may not have been a wise move, situated as it was under a large snow-laden fir. Then there was a loud whooshing sound and an explosion as a dump truck-load of snow made a direct hit on the fire. The snow bomb filled my cozy den with ash and burning cinders, and filled the air with ice crystals, making it impossible to breathe.

I huddled against the tree trunk until daylight, listening to the snow bombs falling all around and waiting for another direct hit. At dawn, I rebuilt the fire. I just got it going when another snow bomb fell and extinguished it. I dug my soggy gear out of what was left of my lean-to, wrapped it in a ball of wet plastic and slogged out to the open bank of the river.

I had almost made it out from under the trees when I was knocked off my feet by another snow bomb. I crawled under a cut bank along the river. Luckily, I still had my rod, so I cast up into the hole. There was a strike, then a silver flash in the blue water. I wanted to cook that fish and eat it, but I would have had to build a fire.

A Lonely River

The water filled the river
The river shaped the land.
The land has been forever
The history of man.
One night has turned another
Sky a scarlet band.
I'm on a lonely river.
I try to understand.

Shadowed in the timber.
The river voices flow.
And cause me to remember
A hundred years ago.
The people were together
Their fire was burning low.
I'm on a lonely river.
The only one I know.

They started in the morning
Before the break of day.
The current set them moving
And swept a world away.
A ghostly fleet a sailing
No wish could make them stay.

A lonely river winding.
That's where I'll end my day.

Guide Grudge

It was daylight on the river. A frozen rain was turning to snow, and a southwest gale pushed the treetops in awkward circles. There were white caps on the mud puddles in the parking lot where I huddled in my truck. I was waiting for my client to get out of the outhouse. I had to find out just how desperate he was to catch a steelhead. Drifting our rivers in a windstorm can be a religious experience, with the trees falling and spray from the rapids blowing upstream in a solid sheet of misery.

With any luck at all the client would cancel the trip and I could get back home in time for my soap operas. But I had to wait for the guy to get out of the outhouse. It was the professional thing to do.

After a while, the poor guy staggered out looking like he'd lost his best friend. He'd dropped his wallet in the outhouse. And when he bent over to look, his cell phone fell out of his pocket into the same unforgiving hole.

What could I do but loan the guy a fly rod and a big, floating, wet fly pattern, the Dungeness Special. He went back into the outhouse for his own private fishing derby. It might have been the only dry spot there was to fish that day.

My guide instincts told me if he didn't snag his wallet I wouldn't get paid. I waited around and watched the outhouse derby. It was the professional thing to do.

I heard a cough like a sick animal would make. There in the wind and hail was an extremely large fisherman perched on top of a small motorcycle that did not want to start. That may have been a lucky break. The guy had launched upstream then drove his truck and trailer down-river to the bottom of the drift. He must have figured on riding the scooter back up to his boat for a day's fishing. It's a bad idea to ride a motor scooter on Highway 101 even when it's *not* snowing.

I asked the guy if he had a death wish or wanted a ride.

"Sure," he said, throwing the bike into the back of his truck like it was so much scrap metal. He got in my truck and lit a cigar.

"I come up here to get away from fishing guides." He said. "I hate them. They think they own the river."

"Me too," I said.

He went on to explain the many bloody feuds he'd had with fishing guides out on the west end of the Olympic Peninsula. He hated fishing guides so much, he had stuffed potatoes up their exhaust pipes, poured sugar in their gas tanks, or just plain punched them out from one river to the next.

I don't know why, but I said, "You should put salt peter in the whiskey if you really want to hurt the fishing guides."

The guy was obviously a dangerous psychopath. I noticed a bulge in his jacket where a shoulder holster would be. He pulled out a beer and offered one to me. I said no, thanks—I was driving. It was 7 AM.

"Nothing like that first beer in the morning he said." He finished that first beer as we crossed a bridge over the Sol Duc River.

"There's a stinking fishing guide now!" the psychopath yelled, throwing the empty beer bottle out the window of my truck.

I was a marked man. Fishing guides are sensitive woodland creatures. You almost don't have to throw a beer bottle at a fishing guide to upset them. I knew there would be retribution. The old Good Samaritan-gone-bad excuse would not fly. I needed to take a long vacation somewhere else or change vehicles and get some plastic surgery to keep fishing locally.

But that would come later. For now, it was enough to pour the psycho back into his boat.

He thanked me profusely for giving him a ride in the snowstorm, then reached into his coat. I figured this was the part of the tale where I would get shot. He pulled out a potato—a big number one baker—and then, cursing a guide, parked near the boat ramp and said, "This spud's for you. Oh, by the way, what do you do for work?"

"I am a journalist," I replied carefully. "A journalist on assignment." I drove away. It felt good to be alive.

Guide School

These days, it seems as if there's a whole new generation of fishing guides clogging up the river. It's shameful the way the new guys launch late in the morning, fake bites just to make their clients think there's fish around, and then make excuses for getting skunked. Little gems like, "You should have been here a hundred years ago ..."

I figured I might as well sell my guide secrets before they were all stolen, so I started a guide school. Guiding may not be the world's oldest profession, but it's a close second. Jesus was the first fishing guide in recorded history. He was always fishing, or whipping up a fish shore lunch for hungry crowds.

One of his guys caught a fish with a gold coin in its mouth. That's the last time I've heard of anyone making any easy money fishing.

And Jesus knew how to handle a boat. If things got really rough, he could calm the storm.

Maybe you've been there, out of sight of land. The decks are awash. The mast is broken. The skipper and crew are homicidal, suicidal, drunk, or any combination of the three. You look up into the crests of the waves and down to the bottom of the sea. You are in the hand of God. That's when generations of fishermen have prayed to Jesus, the only guide who could ever walk on water.

The Bible tells us Jesus died, rose from the dead, and went fishing. He was cooking a shore lunch when the rest of the crew drifted in. They'd been fishing all night. They were skunked. That's when Jesus gave us the best fishing advice ever: fish off the right side of the boat. I can tell you from years' of experience in fishing off the *wrong* side of the boat that you really should listen to your guide.

Fishing has gotten a whole lot worse since Jesus. His high standards of guide professionalism have slid way downhill. These days, it might be easier for a bull elk to get through the eye of a fishhook than a fishing guide to get into heaven. Nevertheless, it's like we say on the river: the worse fishing gets, the more you need a guide.

Being a fishing guide takes a lot more than a big hat, a tin boat, and a riot gun. You need bungee cords, duct tape, and people skills to deal with today's sport angler.

My guide school courses teach you how guide fly fishermen. These are people who use the fur and feathers of endangered species to catch an endangered trout so they can let it go. Their goal is not necessarily to catch a fish, but to see how far they can cast.

Fly fishermen are encouraged to use barbless hooks. There's less bleeding and it makes for a much easier release when they snag the guide.

You'll learn how to fish with bait fishermen. These are people who think fishing is a form of water pollution. They don't mind smelling like the dumpster behind a fish market as they hook up globs of rotten fish eggs, shrimp, and herring to throw in our pristine waters. Bait fishermen are encouraged to stay downwind.

We cover the secrets of fishing spinners and spoons. For example, don't cast your gear up in the trees. While they do put up a heck of a fight, the fish aren't up there—at least not until the water gets higher.

My fishing guide school covers everything from first aid (check for wallet) to the secrets of wilderness cooking (don't).

I don't know, maybe they saw it on TV somewhere: a guide cooking. I remember one time a client asked me to make him a sandwich. I told him, "We're not married, so you can't talk to me that way."

Besides, I'm the guy rigging up rotten globs of fish eggs, shrimp, and herring all day. Do you really want me anywhere near your food?

Experiments with cooking on board a drift boat have been disastrous. The combination of a barbecue and a boat is a recipe for disaster. Whitewater barbecuing will never catch on big in this country.

If forced to cook, stick to the basic food groups: chili. Serve chili three meals a day until someone complains and, viola, they're the new camp cook.

We'll share a rich tradition of client-hazing rituals passed down by fishing guides through the ages. You'll learn the old guides' secrets to catching bigger fish. My guide model scale is specially calibrated to make any fish weigh up to 25 percent more. My guide model tape measure can add inches to any fish.

Most importantly, my guide school will help you translate our nation's complex fishing laws into English. That alone is worth the price of tuition.

For whatever reason, I had trouble attracting students for my guide school. I had to take what I could get. Like the bunch that showed up that Saturday morning. I knew they were trouble when one of them said, "I don't have a fishing license."

"That's okay," I said. "You don't need a fishing license to go poaching."

"What's poaching?" another class member asked.

Apparently, these kids didn't get out much. They were from the Ronald McDonald House, which is a home away from home for children being treated at Children's Hospital in Seattle. One of the students had already dropped out of the guide school; he died waiting to go fishing. We didn't have time for the season to open. We were going poaching.

"Are we going to catch a hundred-pound salmon?" one of the kids asked. Now *there's* a question I dread. The Spanish explorer Manuel Quimper bought some hundred-pound salmon from the Indians off the mouth of the Elwha River back in July 1790. People have been coming to the Olympic Peninsula to catch a hundred-pound salmon ever since.

But what could I say? They should have been here 200 years ago? I sell dreams, and I wasn't about to stomp on someone else's just to be a know it all. I told the kids it was a good day to try.

We pulled into one of the best fishing holes around, a pond stocked with big rainbow trout and just enough hundred-pound salmon thrown in to make it interesting. Hey, you never know.

Maybe I said a lot of stuff. Like, that the pond belonged to an old sea captain with a hook, a wooden leg full of rum, and a bloodshot eye in the back of his head. He only left home one day a year to go to the tugboat races, and today was the day.

What was I supposed to do? Tell the truth, that sea captain had a heart as big as that pond? He told me to let those kids catch all the fish they wanted. Our student guides represent the hopes and dreams of the future. I think we owe them more than the truth. We were poaching that pond, ready to scatter into the brush if the sea captain returned home while we were there.

I handed out the poles and tied on a fly pattern of my own design: the sinking bread fly. Then it was "Fish on!" Everybody caught a limit, whatever that meant.

And the sea captain wasn't home yet. We made a clean getaway up into the hills. I showed the student guides how to build a campfire and keep it under an acre. We cooked the fish on alder coals. They said it was just like home. It's the best tip a guide ever got.

One of the boys was a two-fer. He had lymphoma and leukemia. Another boy had a disease I couldn't pronounce, and more side-effects than you could shake a fishing pole at. They were okay, the last I heard. They spent their days getting ready to go fishing again. Maybe they were so busy getting their gear ready that nothing else mattered.

Fishing may not be a matter of life and death. Maybe it's much more important than that.

978-0-595-44467-
0-595-44467-9

LaVergne, TN USA
03 December 2010
207242LV00005B/54/A